Travel phrasebooks collect
«Everything Will Be Okay

M000235109

PHRASEBOOK

— RUSSIAN —

By Andrey Taranov

THE MOST IMPORTANT PHRASES

This phrasebook contains
the most important
phrases and questions
for basic communication
Everything you need
to survive overseas

T&P BOOKS

Phrasebook + 250-word dictionary

English-Russian phrasebook & mini dictionary

By Andrey Taranov

The collection of "Everything Will Be Okay" travel phrasebooks published by T&P Books is designed for people traveling abroad for tourism and business. The phrasebooks contain what matters most - the essentials for basic communication. This is an indispensable set of phrases to "survive" while abroad.

You'll also find a mini dictionary with 250 useful words required for everyday communication - the names of months and days of the week, measurements, family members, and more.

T&P Books Publishing
www.tpbooks.com

ISBN: 978-1-78492-403-4

This book is also available in E-book formats.
Please visit www.tpbooks.com or the major online bookstores.

FOREWORD

The collection of "Everything Will Be Okay" travel phrasebooks published by T&P Books is designed for people traveling abroad for tourism and business. The phrasebooks contain what matters most - the essentials for basic communication. This is an indispensable set of phrases to "survive" while abroad.

This phrasebook will help you in most cases where you need to ask something, get directions, find out how much something costs, etc. It can also resolve difficult communication situations where gestures just won't help.

This book contains a lot of phrases that have been grouped according to the most relevant topics. You'll also find a mini dictionary with useful words - numbers, time, calendar, colors...

Take "Everything Will Be Okay" phrasebook with you on the road and you'll have an irreplaceable traveling companion who will help you find your way out of any situation and teach you to not fear speaking with foreigners.

TABLE OF CONTENTS

T&P Books Publishing

PRONUNCIATION

Letter	Russian example	T&P phonetic alphabet	English example
А, а	трава	[ɑ], [a]	bath, to pass
Е, е	перерыв	[e]	elm, medal
Ё, ё	ёлка	[jɔ:], [ɜ:]	yourself, girl
И, и	филин	[i], [i:]	feet, Peter
О, о	корова	[o], [o:]	floor, doctor
У, у	Тулуза	[u], [u:]	book, shoe
Э, э	эволюция	[ɛ]	man, bad
Ю, ю	трюм	[ju:], [ju]	cued, cute
Я, я	яблоко	[ja:], [æ:]	royal
Б, б	баобаб	[b]	baby, book
В, в	врач, вино	[v]	very, river
Г, г	глагол	[g]	game, gold
Д, д	дом, труд	[d]	day, doctor
Ж, ж	живот	[ʒ]	forge, pleasure
З, з	зоопарк	[z]	zebra, please
Й, й	йога	[j]	yes, New York
ой	стройка	[ɔj]	oil, boy, point
ай	край	[aj]	time, white
К, к	кино, сок	[k]	clock, kiss
Л, л	лопата	[l]	lace, people
М, м	март, сом	[m]	magic, milk
Н, н	небо	[n]	name, normal
П, п	папа	[p]	pencil, private
Р, р	урок, робот	[r]	rice, radio
С, с	собака	[s]	city, boss
Т, т	ток, стая	[t]	tourist, trip
Ф, ф	фарфор	[f]	face, food
Х, х	хобот, страх	[h]	home, have
Ц, ц	цапля	[ts]	cats, tsetse fly
Ч, ч	чемодан	[tʃ]	church, French
Ш, ш	шум, шашки	[ʃ]	machine, shark
Щ, щ	щенок	[ɕ]	sheep, shop
Ы, ы	рыба	[ɪ]	big, America

Letter	Russian example	T&P phonetic alphabet	English example
Ь, ь	дверь	[ʲ]	soft sign - no sound
нь	конь	[ɲ]	canyon, new
ль	соль	[ʎ]	daily, million
ть	статья	[t]	tune, student
Ъ, ъ	подъезд	[ˮ]	hard sign - no sound

LIST OF ABBREVIATIONS

English abbreviations

ab.	-	about
adj	-	adjective
adv	-	adverb
anim.	-	animate
as adj	-	attributive noun used as adjective
e.g.	-	for example
etc.	-	et cetera
fam.	-	familiar
fem.	-	feminine
form.	-	formal
inanim.	-	inanimate
masc.	-	masculine
math	-	mathematics
mil.	-	military
n	-	noun
pl	-	plural
pron.	-	pronoun
sb	-	somebody
sing.	-	singular
sth	-	something
v aux	-	auxiliary verb
vi	-	intransitive verb
vi, vt	-	intransitive, transitive verb
vt	-	transitive verb

Russian abbreviations

ж	-	feminine noun
ж мн	-	feminine plural
м	-	masculine noun
м мн	-	masculine plural
м, ж	-	masculine, feminine
мн	-	plural
с	-	neuter
с мн	-	neuter plural

RUSSIAN PHRASEBOOK

This section contains
important phrases that may
come in handy in various
real-life situations.
The phrasebook will help
you ask for directions, clarify
a price, buy tickets, and
order food at a restaurant

T&P Books Publishing

PHRASEBOOK
CONTENTS

T&P Books Publishing

The bare minimum

Excuse me, ...
Извините, ...
[izwiˈnite, ...]

Hello.
Здравствуйте.
[ˈzdrastvʊjte]

Thank you.
Спасибо.
[spaˈsibə]

Good bye.
До свидания.
[da swiˈdanija]

Yes.
Да.
[da]

No.
Нет.
[net]

I don't know.
Я не знаю.
[ja ne ˈznaⁱʉ]

Where? | Where to? | When?
Где? | Куда? | Когда?
[gde? | kʊˈda? | kagˈda?]

I need ...
Мне нужен ...
[mne ˈnʊʒən ...]

I want ...
Я хочу ...
[ja haˈʧu ...]

Do you have ...?
У вас есть ...?
[u vas estʲ ...?]

Is there a ... here?
Здесь есть ...?
[zdesʲ estʲ ...?]

May I ...?
Я могу ...?
[ja maˈgʊ ...?]

..., please (polite request)
пожалуйста
[paˈʒaləstə]

I'm looking for ...
Я ищу ...
[ja iˈɕu ...]

restroom
туалет
[tʊaˈlet]

ATM
банкомат
[bankaˈmat]

pharmacy (drugstore)
аптеку
[apˈtekʊ]

hospital
больницу
[balʲˈnitsu]

police station
полицейский участок
[paliˈtsɛjskij uˈʧastək]

subway
метро
[metˈrɔ]

taxi	**такси** [tak'si]
train station	**вокзал** [vak'zal]

My name is …	**Меня зовут …** [mi'ɲa za'vʊt …]
What's your name?	**Как вас зовут?** [kak vas za'vʊt?]
Could you please help me?	**Помогите мне, пожалуйста.** [pama'gite mne, pa'ʒaləstə]
I've got a problem.	**У меня проблема.** [u me'ɲa prab'lema]
I don't feel well.	**Мне плохо.** [mne 'plɔhə]
Call an ambulance!	**Вызовите скорую!** [vɪzawite 'skɔrʊʲʊ!]
May I make a call?	**Могу я позвонить?** [ma'gʊ ja pazva'nitʲ?]

I'm sorry.	**Извините.** [izwi'nite]
You're welcome.	**Пожалуйста.** [pa'ʒaləstə]

I, me	**я** [ja]
you (inform.)	**ты** [tɪ]
he	**он** [ɔn]
she	**она** [a'na]
they (masc.)	**они** [a'ni]
they (fem.)	**они** [a'ni]
we	**мы** [mɪ]
you (pl)	**вы** [vɪ]
you (sg, form.)	**Вы** [vɪ]

ENTRANCE	**ВХОД** [vhɔt]
EXIT	**ВЫХОД** ['vɪhət]
OUT OF ORDER	**НЕ РАБОТАЕТ** [ne ra'botaet]
CLOSED	**ЗАКРЫТО** [zak'rɪtə]

OPEN	**ОТКРЫТО** [atk'rɪtə]
FOR WOMEN	**ДЛЯ ЖЕНЩИН** [dʌa 'ʒɛnçin]
FOR MEN	**ДЛЯ МУЖЧИН** [dʌa mʊ'çin]

Questions

Where?	**Где?** [gde?]
Where to?	**Куда?** [kʊ'da?]
Where from?	**Откуда?** [at'kʊda?]
Why?	**Почему?** [patʃe'mʊ?]
For what reason?	**Зачем?** [za'tʃem?]
When?	**Когда?** [kag'da?]

How long?	**Как долго?** [kak 'dɔlga?]
At what time?	**Во сколько?** [va 'skɔlʲkə?]
How much?	**Сколько стоит?** ['skɔlʲkə 'stɔit?]
Do you have ...?	**У вас есть ...?** [u vas estʲ ...?]
Where is ...?	**Где находится ...?** [gde na'hɔditsa ...?]

What time is it?	**Который час?** [ka'tɔrɪj tʃas?]
May I make a call?	**Могу я позвонить?** [ma'gʊ ja pazva'nitʲ?]
Who's there?	**Кто там?** [kto tam?]
Can I smoke here?	**Могу я здесь курить?** [ma'gʊ ja zdesʲ kʊ'ritʲ?]
May I ...?	**Я могу ...?** [ja ma'gʊ ...?]

Needs

I'd like ...
Я бы хотел /хотела/ ...
[ja bɪ ha'tel /ha'tela/ ...]

I don't want ...
Я не хочу ...
[ja ne ha'ʧu ...]

I'm thirsty.
Я хочу пить.
[ja ha'ʧu pitʲ]

I want to sleep.
Я хочу спать.
[ja ha'ʧu spatʲ]

I want ...
Я хочу ...
[ja ha'ʧu ...]

to wash up
умыться
[u'mɪʦa]

to brush my teeth
почистить зубы
[pa'ʧistitʲ 'zubɪ]

to rest a while
немного отдохнуть
[nem'nɔgə atdah'nutʲ]

to change my clothes
переодеться
[perea'deʦa]

to go back to the hotel
вернуться в гостиницу
[wer'nuʦa v gas'tiniʦu]

to buy ...
купить ...
[ku'pitʲ ...]

to go to ...
съездить в ...
[sʲʲezditʲ v ...]

to visit ...
посетить ...
[pasi'titʲ ...]

to meet with ...
встретиться с ...
[vstrʲetiʦa s ...]

to make a call
позвонить
[pazva'nitʲ]

I'm tired.
Я устал /устала/.
[ja us'tal /us'tala/]

We are tired.
Мы устали.
[mɪ us'tali]

I'm cold.
Мне холодно.
[mne 'hɔladnə]

I'm hot.
Мне жарко.
[mne 'ʒarkə]

I'm OK.
Мне нормально.
[mne nar'malʲnə]

I need to make a call.

Мне надо позвонить.
[mne 'nada pazva'nit']

I need to go to the restroom.

Мне надо в туалет.
[mne 'nada v tua'let]

I have to go.

Мне пора.
[mne pa'ra]

I have to go now.

Мне надо идти.
[mne 'nada it'ti]

Asking for directions

Excuse me, ...

Извините, ...
[izwi'nite, ...]

Where is ...?

Где находится ...?
[gde na'hoditsa ...?]

Which way is ...?

В каком направлении находится ...?
[v ka'kom naprav'lenii na'hoditsa ...?]

Could you help me, please?

Помогите мне, пожалуйста.
[pama'gite mne, pa'ʒaləstə]

I'm looking for ...

Я ищу ...
[ja i'ɕu ...]

I'm looking for the exit.

Я ищу выход.
[ja i'ɕu 'vɪhət]

I'm going to ...

Я еду в ...
[ja 'edʊ v ...]

Am I going the right way to ...?

Я правильно иду ...?
[ja 'prawilʲnə i'dʊ ...?]

Is it far?

Это далеко?
['ɛtə dale'kɔ?]

Can I get there on foot?

Я дойду туда пешком?
[ja daj'dʊ tʊ'da peʃ'kɔm?]

Can you show me on the map?

Покажите мне на карте, пожалуйста.
[paka'ʒite mne na 'karte, pa'ʒaləstə]

Show me where we are right now.

Покажите, где мы сейчас.
[paka'ʒite, gde mɪ se'tʃas]

Here

Здесь
[zdesʲ]

There

Там
[tam]

This way

Сюда
[sʲʊ'da]

Turn right.

Поверните направо.
[pawer'nite nap'ravə]

Turn left.

Поверните налево.
[pawer'nite na'levə]

first (second, third) turn

первый (второй, третий) поворот
['pervɪj (vta'rɔj, 'tretij) pava'rɔt]

to the right

направо
[nap'ravə]

to the left

налево
[na'levə]

Go straight.

Идите прямо.
[i'dite 'prʲamə]

Signs

WELCOME!	**ДОБРО ПОЖАЛОВАТЬ!** [dab'rɔ pa'ʒalavətʲ!]
ENTRANCE	**ВХОД** [vhɔt]
EXIT	**ВЫХОД** ['vɪhət]

PUSH	**ОТ СЕБЯ** [at se'bʲa]
PULL	**НА СЕБЯ** [na se'bʲa]
OPEN	**ОТКРЫТО** [atk'rɪtə]
CLOSED	**ЗАКРЫТО** [zak'rɪtə]

FOR WOMEN	**ДЛЯ ЖЕНЩИН** [dʎa 'ʒɛnɕin]
FOR MEN	**ДЛЯ МУЖЧИН** [dʎa mu'ɕin]
MEN, GENTS	**МУЖСКОЙ ТУАЛЕТ** [muʃs'kɔj tua'let]
WOMEN, LADIES	**ЖЕНСКИЙ ТУАЛЕТ** [ʒɛnskij tua'let]

DISCOUNTS	**СКИДКИ** ['skitki]
SALE	**РАСПРОДАЖА** [raspra'daʒa]
FREE	**БЕСПЛАТНО** [bisp'latnə]
NEW!	**НОВИНКА!** [na'vinka!]
ATTENTION!	**ВНИМАНИЕ!** [vni'maniə!]

NO VACANCIES	**МЕСТ НЕТ** [mest 'net]
RESERVED	**ЗАРЕЗЕРВИРОВАНО** [zarizer'wiravanə]
ADMINISTRATION	**АДМИНИСТРАЦИЯ** [administ'ratsija]
STAFF ONLY	**ТОЛЬКО ДЛЯ ПЕРСОНАЛА** [tɔlʲkə dʎa persa'nala]

BEWARE OF THE DOG!	**ЗЛАЯ СОБАКА** ['zlaja sa'baka]
NO SMOKING!	**НЕ КУРИТЬ!** [ne kʊ'ritʲ!]
DO NOT TOUCH!	**РУКАМИ НЕ ТРОГАТЬ!** [rʊ'kami ne 'trogatʲ!]
DANGEROUS	**ОПАСНО** [a'pasnə]
DANGER	**ОПАСНОСТЬ** [a'pasnəstʲ]
HIGH VOLTAGE	**ВЫСОКОЕ НАПРЯЖЕНИЕ** [vɪ'sokae napri'ʒɛnie]
NO SWIMMING!	**КУПАТЬСЯ ЗАПРЕЩЕНО** [kʊ'patsa zapriɕe'nɔ!]

OUT OF ORDER	**НЕ РАБОТАЕТ** [ne ra'botaet]
FLAMMABLE	**ОГНЕОПАСНО** [agnea'pasnə]
FORBIDDEN	**ЗАПРЕЩЕНО** [zapriɕe'nɔ]
NO TRESPASSING!	**ПРОХОД ЗАПРЕЩЁН** [pra'hot zapri'ɕon!]
WET PAINT	**ОКРАШЕНО** [ak'raʃənə]

CLOSED FOR RENOVATIONS	**ЗАКРЫТО НА РЕМОНТ** [zak'rɪtə na re'mont]
WORKS AHEAD	**РЕМОНТНЫЕ РАБОТЫ** [re'montnɪe ra'botɪ]
DETOUR	**ОБЪЕЗД** [abʰ'ezt]

Transportation. General phrases

plane	**самолёт** [sama'lʲot]
train	**поезд** ['pɔest]
bus	**автобус** [aft'ɔbʊs]
ferry	**паром** [pa'rɔm]
taxi	**такси** [tak'si]
car	**машина** [ma'ʃina]

schedule	**расписание** [raspi'sanie]
Where can I see the schedule?	**Где можно посмотреть расписание?** [gde 'mɔʒnə pasmat'retʲ raspi'sanie?]
workdays (weekdays)	**рабочие дни** [ra'bɔtʃie dni]
weekends	**выходные дни** [vɪhad'nɪe dni]
holidays	**праздничные дни** ['prazdnitʃnɪe dni]

DEPARTURE	**ОТПРАВЛЕНИЕ** [atprav'lenie]
ARRIVAL	**ПРИБЫТИЕ** [pri'bɪtie]
DELAYED	**ЗАДЕРЖИВАЕТСЯ** [za'derʒivaetsa]
CANCELED	**ОТМЕНЕН** [atme'nʲon]

next (train, etc.)	**следующий** ['sledʊɕij]
first	**первый** ['pervɪj]
last	**последний** [pas'lednij]

When is the next ...?	**Когда будет следующий ...?** [kag'da 'bʊdet 'sledʊɕij ...?]
When is the first ...?	**Когда отходит первый ...?** [kag'da at'hɔdit 'pervɪj ...?]

When is the last ...?

Когда уходит последний ...?
[kag'da u'hɔdit pas'lednij ...?]

transfer (change of trains, etc.)

пересадка
[piri'satka]

to make a transfer

сделать пересадку
['sdelatʲ piri'satkʊ]

Do I need to make a transfer?

Мне нужно делать пересадку?
[mne 'nuʒnə 'delatʲ piri'satkʊ?]

Buying tickets

Where can I buy tickets?

Где можно купить билеты?
[gde 'moʒnə kʊ'pitʲ bi'letɪ?]

ticket

билет
[bi'let]

to buy a ticket

купить билет
[kʊ'pitʲ bi'let]

ticket price

стоимость билета
[stɔiməstʲ bi'leta]

Where to?

Куда?
[kʊ'da?]

To what station?

До какой станции?
[do ka'kɔj 'stantsii?]

I need ...

Мне нужно ...
[mne 'nʊʒnə ...]

one ticket

один билет
[a'din bi'let]

two tickets

два билета
[dva bi'leta]

three tickets

три билета
[tri bi'leta]

one-way

в один конец
[v a'din ka'nets]

round-trip

туда и обратно
[tʊ'da i ab'ratnə]

first class

первый класс
['pervɪj klass]

second class

второй класс
[fta'rɔj klass]

today

сегодня
[si'vɔdɲa]

tomorrow

завтра
['zaftra]

the day after tomorrow

послезавтра
[pɔsle'zaftra]

in the morning

утром
['utrəm]

in the afternoon

днём
[dnʲom]

in the evening

вечером
['wetʃerəm]

aisle seat

место у прохода
['mestə u pra'hɔda]

window seat

место у окна
['mestə u ak'na]

How much?

Сколько?
['skolʲkə?]

Can I pay by credit card?

Могу я заплатить карточкой?
[ma'gʊ ja zapla'titʲ 'kartəʧkəj?]

Bus

bus	**автобус** [aft'ɔbʊs]
intercity bus	**междугородний автобус** [meʒdʊga'rɔdnij aft'ɔbʊs]
bus stop	**автобусная остановка** [aft'ɔbʊsnaja asta'nɔfka]
Where's the nearest bus stop?	**Где ближайшая автобусная остановка?** [gde bli'ʒajʃəja aft'ɔbʊsnaja asta'nɔfka?]
number (bus ~, etc.)	**номер** ['nɔmer]
Which bus do I take to get to ...?	**Какой автобус идёт до ...?** [ka'kɔj aft'ɔbʊs i'dʲot dɔ ...?]
Does this bus go to ...?	**Этот автобус идёт до ...?** [ɛtət av'tɔbʊs i'dʲot dɔ ...?]
How frequent are the buses?	**Как часто ходят автобусы?** [kak 'tʃastə 'hɔdʲat aft'ɔbʊsɪ?]
every 15 minutes	**каждые 15 минут** ['kaʒdɪe pit'natsatʲ mi'nʊt]
every half hour	**каждые полчаса** ['kaʒdɪe pɔltʃa'sa]
every hour	**каждый час** ['kaʒdɪj tʃas]
several times a day	**несколько раз в день** ['neskalʲkə raz v denʲ]
... times a day	**... раз в день** [... raz v denʲ]
schedule	**расписание** [raspi'sanie]
Where can I see the schedule?	**Где можно посмотреть расписание?** [gde 'mɔʒnə pasmat'retʲ raspi'sanie?]
When is the next bus?	**Когда будет следующий автобус?** [kag'da 'bʊdet 'sledʊɕij aft'ɔbʊs?]
When is the first bus?	**Когда отходит первый автобус?** [kag'da at'hɔdit 'pervɪj aft'ɔbʊs?]
When is the last bus?	**Когда уходит последний автобус?** [kag'da u'hɔdit pas'lednij aft'ɔbʊs?]
stop	**остановка** [asta'nɔfka]

next stop

следующая остановка
['sledʋɕəja asta'nɔfka]

last stop (terminus)

конечная остановка
[ka'netʃnəja asta'nɔfka]

Stop here, please.

Остановите здесь, пожалуйста.
[astana'wite zdesʲ, pa'ʒaləstə]

Excuse me, this is my stop.

Разрешите, это моя остановка.
[razre'ʃite, 'ɛtə ma'ja asta'nɔfka]

Train

train	поезд
	['poest]
suburban train	пригородный поезд
	['prigəradnɪj 'poest]
long-distance train	поезд дальнего следования
	['poest 'dalʲnevə 'sledavanɪja]
train station	вокзал
	[vak'zal]
Excuse me, where is the exit to the platform?	Извините, где выход к поездам?
	[izwi'nite, gde 'vɪhət k paez'dam?]

Does this train go to ...?	Этот поезд идёт до ...?
	[ɛtət 'poest i'dʲot do ...?]
next train	следующий поезд
	['sledʊɕij 'poest]
When is the next train?	Когда будет следующий поезд?
	[kag'da 'bʊdet 'sledʊɕij 'poest?]
Where can I see the schedule?	Где можно посмотреть расписание?
	[gde 'moʒnə pasmat'retʲ raspi'sanie?]
From which platform?	С какой платформы?
	[s ka'koj plat'formɪ?]
When does the train arrive in ...?	Когда поезд прибывает в ...?
	[kag'da 'poest pribɪ'vaet v ...?]

Please help me.	Помогите мне, пожалуйста.
	[pama'gite mne, pa'ʒaləstə]
I'm looking for my seat.	Я ищу своё место.
	[ja i'ɕu sva'jo 'mestə]
We're looking for our seats.	Мы ищем наши места.
	[mɪ 'iɕem 'naʃi mes'ta]
My seat is taken.	Моё место занято.
	[ma'jo 'mestə 'zaɲatə]
Our seats are taken.	Наши места заняты.
	['naʃi mes'ta 'zaɲatɪ]

I'm sorry but this is my seat.	Извините, пожалуйста, но это моё место.
	[izwi'nite, pa'ʒaləstə, no 'ɛtə ma'ʲo 'mestə]
Is this seat taken?	Это место свободно?
	[ɛtə 'mestə sva'bodnə?]
May I sit here?	Могу я здесь сесть?
	[ma'gʊ ja zdesʲ 'sestʲ?]

On the train. Dialogue (No ticket)

Ticket, please.
Ваш билет, пожалуйста.
[vaʃ bi'let, pa'ʒaləstə]

I don't have a ticket.
У меня нет билета.
[u me'ɲa net bi'leta]

I lost my ticket.
Я потерял /потеряла/ свой билет.
[ja pate'rʲal /pate'rʲala/ svɔj bi'let]

I forgot my ticket at home.
Я забыл /забыла/ билет дома.
[ja za'bɪl /za'bɪla/ bi'let 'dɔma]

You can buy a ticket from me.
Вы можете купить билет у меня.
[vɪ 'mɔʒɛte kʊ'pitʲ bi'let u me'ɲa]

You will also have to pay a fine.
Вам ещё придётся заплатить штраф.
[vam i'ɕʲo pri'dʲoʦa zapla'titʲ 'ʃtraf]

Okay.
Хорошо.
[hara'ʃɔ]

Where are you going?
Куда вы едете?
[kʊ'da vɪ 'edete?]

I'm going to …
Я еду до …
[ja 'edʊ dɔ …]

How much? I don't understand.
Сколько? Я не понимаю.
['skɔlʲkə? ja ne pani'maʲʉ]

Write it down, please.
Напишите, пожалуйста.
[napi'ʃite, pa'ʒaləstə]

Okay. Can I pay with a credit card?
Хорошо. Могу я заплатить карточкой?
[hara'ʃɔ. ma'gʊ ja zapla'titʲ 'kartətʃkəj?]

Yes, you can.
Да, можете.
[da 'mɔʒɛte]

Here's your receipt.
Вот ваша квитанция.
[vɔt 'vaʃʌ kwi'tanʦija]

Sorry about the fine.
Сожалею о штрафе.
[saʒə'leʲʉ ɔ 'ʃtrafe]

That's okay. It was my fault.
Это ничего. Это моя вина.
['ɛtə nitʃe'vɔ. 'ɛtə ma'ja wi'na]

Enjoy your trip.
Приятной вам поездки.
[pri'jatnəj vam pa'eztki]

Taxi

taxi	**такси** [tak'si]
taxi driver	**таксист** [tak'sist]
to catch a taxi	**поймать такси** [paj'matʲ tak'si]
taxi stand	**стоянка такси** [sta'janka tak'si]
Where can I get a taxi?	**Где я могу взять такси?** [gde ja ma'gʊ vzʲatʲ tak'si?]
to call a taxi	**вызвать такси** ['vizvatʲ tak'si]
I need a taxi.	**Мне нужно такси.** [mne 'nʊʒnə tak'si]
Right now.	**Прямо сейчас.** ['prʲamə se'ʧas]
What is your address (location)?	**Ваш адрес?** [vaʃ 'adres?]
My address is ...	**Мой адрес ...** [mɔj 'adres ...]
Your destination?	**Куда вы поедете?** [kʊ'da vɪ pɔ'edete?]
Excuse me, ...	**Извините, ...** [izwi'nite, ...]
Are you available?	**Вы свободны?** [vɪ sva'bɔdnɪ?]
How much is it to get to ...?	**Сколько стоит доехать до ...?** ['skɔlʲkə 'stɔit da'ehatʲ dɔ ...?]
Do you know where it is?	**Вы знаете, где это?** [vɪ 'znaete, 'gde ɛtɔ?]
Airport, please.	**В аэропорт, пожалуйста.** [v aɛra'pɔrt, pa'ʒaləstə]
Stop here, please.	**Остановитесь здесь, пожалуйста.** [astana'witesʲ zdesʲ, pa'ʒaləstə]
It's not here.	**Это не здесь.** ['ɛtə ne zdesʲ]
This is the wrong address.	**Это неправильный адрес.** ['ɛtə nep'rawilʲnɪj 'adres]
Turn left.	**Сейчас налево.** [si'ʧas na'levə]
Turn right.	**Сейчас направо.** [si'ʧas nap'ravə]

How much do I owe you?	**Сколько я вам должен /должна/?** ['skolʲkə ja vam 'dolʒen /dolʒ'na/?]
I'd like a receipt, please.	**Дайте мне чек, пожалуйста.** [dajte mne 'ʧek, pa'ʒaləstə]
Keep the change.	**Сдачи не надо.** [sdatʃi ne 'nadə]

Would you please wait for me?	**Подождите меня, пожалуйста.** [padaʒ'dite me'ɲa, pa'ʒaləstə]
five minutes	**5 минут** [pʲatʲ mi'nʊt]
ten minutes	**10 минут** ['desʲatʲ mi'nʊt]
fifteen minutes	**15 минут** [pit'natsatʲ mi'nʊt]
twenty minutes	**20 минут** ['dvatsatʲ mi'nʊt]
half an hour	**полчаса** [poltʃa'sa]

Hotel

Hello.	**Здравствуйте.** ['zdrastvujte]
My name is …	**Меня зовут …** [mi'ɲa za'vut …]
I have a reservation.	**Я резервировал /резервировала/ номер.** [ja rezer'virəval /rezer'virəvala/ 'nɔmer]
I need …	**Мне нужен …** [mne 'nuʒən …]
a single room	**одноместный номер** [ədna'mesnij 'nɔmer]
a double room	**двухместный номер** [dvuh'mesnij 'nɔmer]
How much is that?	**Сколько он стоит?** ['skɔlʲkə ɔn 'stɔit?]
That's a bit expensive.	**Это немного дорого.** [ɛtə nem'nɔgə 'dɔragə]
Do you have any other options?	**У вас есть еще что-нибудь?** [u vas estʲ e'ɕɔ ʃtɔ ni'butʲ?]
I'll take it.	**Я возьму его.** [ja vazʲ'mu e'vɔ]
I'll pay in cash.	**Я заплачу наличными.** [ja zapla'ʧu na'liʧnimi]
I've got a problem.	**У меня проблема.** [u me'ɲa prab'lema]
My … is broken.	**Мой … сломан /Моя … сломана/** [mɔj … 'slɔman /ma'ja … 'slɔmana/]
My … is out of order.	**Мой /Моя/ … не работает.** [mɔj /ma'ja/ … ne ra'bɔtaet]
TV	**телевизор (м)** [tele'wizər]
air conditioning	**кондиционер (м)** [kəndiʦia'ner]
tap	**кран (м)** [kran]
shower	**душ (м)** [duʃ]
sink	**раковина (ж)** ['rakəwina]

safe	сейф (м)
	[sɛjf]
door lock	замок (м)
	[za'mɔk]
electrical outlet	розетка (ж)
	[ra'zetka]
hairdryer	фен (м)
	[fen]

I don't have …	У меня нет …
	[u me'ɲa net …]
water	воды
	[va'dɪ]
light	света
	['sweta]
electricity	электричества
	[ɛlekt'riʧestva]

Can you give me …?	Можете мне дать …?
	['mɔʒete mne datʲ …?]
a towel	полотенце
	[pala'tenʦe]
a blanket	одеяло
	[ade'jalə]
slippers	тапочки
	['tapəʧki]
a robe	халат
	[ha'lat]
shampoo	шампунь
	[ʃʌm'puɲʲ]
soap	мыло
	['mɪlə]

I'd like to change rooms.	Я хотел бы /хотела бы/ поменять номер.
	[ja ha'tel /ha'tela/ bɪ pame'ɲatʲ 'nɔmer]
I can't find my key.	Я не могу найти свой ключ.
	[ja ne ma'gʊ naj'ti svɔj klʲuʧ]
Could you open my room, please?	Откройте мой номер, пожалуйста.
	[atk'rɔjte mɔj 'nɔmer, pa'ʒaləstə]

Who's there?	Кто там?
	[ktɔ tam?]
Come in!	Войдите!
	[vaj'dite!]
Just a minute!	Одну минуту!
	[ad'nʊ mi'nʊtʊ!]
Not right now, please.	Пожалуйста, не сейчас.
	[pa'ʒaləstə, ne se'ʧas]
Come to my room, please.	Зайдите ко мне, пожалуйста.
	[zaj'dite kam'ne, pa'ʒaləstə]

I'd like to order food service.

Я хочу сделать заказ еды в номер.
[ja ha'ʧu 'sdelatʲ za'kas e'dɪ v 'nɔmer]

My room number is …

Мой номер комнаты …
[mɔj 'nɔmer 'kɔmnatɪ …]

I'm leaving …

Я уезжаю …
[ja ue'ʐʐaʲʉ …]

We're leaving …

Мы уезжаем …
[mɪ ue'ʐʐaem …]

right now

сейчас
[se'ʧas]

this afternoon

сегодня после обеда
[se'vɔdɲa 'pɔsle a'beda]

tonight

сегодня вечером
[se'vɔdɲa 'weʧerəm]

tomorrow

завтра
['zaftra]

tomorrow morning

завтра утром
['zaftra 'utrəm]

tomorrow evening

завтра вечером
['zaftra 'weʧerəm]

the day after tomorrow

послезавтра
[pɔsle'zaftra]

I'd like to pay.

Я хотел бы /хотела бы/ рассчитаться.
[ja ha'tel /ha'tela/ bɪ rasɕi'taʦa]

Everything was wonderful.

Всё было отлично.
[vsʲo 'bɪlə at'liʧnə]

Where can I get a taxi?

Где я могу взять такси?
[gde ja ma'gʊ vzʲatʲ tak'si?]

Would you call a taxi for me, please?

Вызовите мне такси, пожалуйста.
[vɪzawite mne tak'si, pa'ʐaləstə]

Restaurant

Can I look at the menu, please?
Могу я посмотреть ваше меню?
[ma'gʊ ja pasmat'retʲ 'vaʃə me'nʲʉ?]

Table for one.
Столик для одного.
[stɔlik dʎa adna'vɔ]

There are two (three, four) of us.
Нас двое (трое, четверо).
[nas 'dvɔe ('trɔe, 'tʃetwerə)]

Smoking
Для курящих
[dʎa kʊ'rʲaɕih]

No smoking
Для некурящих
[dʎa nekʊ'rʲaɕih]

Excuse me! (addressing a waiter)
Будьте добры!
['bʊtʲte dab'rɪ!]

menu
меню
[me'nʲʉ]

wine list
карта вин
['karta win]

The menu, please.
Меню, пожалуйста.
[me'nʲʉ, pa'ʒalestə]

Are you ready to order?
Вы готовы сделать заказ?
[vɪ ga'tɔvɪ 'sdelatʲ za'kas?]

What will you have?
Что вы будете заказывать?
[ʃtɔ vɪ 'bʊdete za'kazɪvatʲ?]

I'll have …
Я буду …
[ja 'bʊdʊ …]

I'm a vegetarian.
Я вегетарианец /вегетарианка/.
[ja wegetari'anets /wegetari'anka/]

meat
мясо
['mʲasə]

fish
рыба
['rɪba]

vegetables
овощи
['ɔvaɕi]

Do you have vegetarian dishes?
У вас есть вегетарианские блюда?
[u vas estʲ wegetari'anskie b'lʲʉda?]

I don't eat pork.
Я не ем свинину.
[ja ne 'em svi'ninʊ]

He /she/ doesn't eat meat.
Он /она/ не ест мясо.
[an /a'na/ ne est 'mʲasə]

I am allergic to …
У меня аллергия на …
[u me'nʲa aler'gija na …]

Would you please bring me ...

Принесите мне, пожалуйста ...
[prine'site mne, pa'ʒaləstə ...]

salt | pepper | sugar

соль | перец | сахар
[sɔlʲ | 'perets | 'sahar]

coffee | tea | dessert

кофе | чай | десерт
['kɔfe | ʧaj | de'sert]

water | sparkling | plain

вода | с газом | без газа
[va'da | s 'gazəm | bes 'gaza]

a spoon | fork | knife

ложка | вилка | нож
['lɔʃka | 'wilka | nɔʃ]

a plate | napkin

тарелка | салфетка
[ta'relka | sal'fetka]

Enjoy your meal!

Приятного аппетита!
[pri'jatnəvə ape'tita!]

One more, please.

Принесите ещё, пожалуйста.
[prine'site e'ɕʲo, pa'ʒaləstə]

It was very delicious.

Было очень вкусно.
['bɪlə 'ɔʧenʲ 'vkusnə]

check | change | tip

счёт | сдача | чаевые
[ɕʲot | 'sdatʃə | ʧəi'vɪe]

Check, please.
(Could I have the check, please?)

Счёт, пожалуйста.
[ɕʲot, pa'ʒaləstə]

Can I pay by credit card?

Могу я заплатить карточкой?
[ma'gu ja zapla'titʲ 'kartətʃkəj?]

I'm sorry, there's a mistake here.

Извините, здесь ошибка.
[izwi'nite, zdesʲ a'ʃɪpka]

Shopping

Can I help you?	**Могу я вам помочь?** [ma'gʊ ja vam pa'mɔtʃ?]
Do you have …?	**У вас есть …?** [u vas estʲ …?]
I'm looking for …	**Я ищу …** [ja i'ɕu …]
I need …	**Мне нужен …** [mne 'nʊʒən …]
I'm just looking.	**Я просто смотрю.** [ja 'prɔstə smat'rʲu]
We're just looking.	**Мы просто смотрим.** [mɪ 'prɔstə 'smɔtrim]
I'll come back later.	**Я зайду позже.** [ja zaj'du 'pɔʑʑə]
We'll come back later.	**Мы зайдём позже.** [mɪ zaj'dʲom 'pɔʑʑə]
discounts	sale	**скидки	распродажа** ['skitki	raspra'daʒa]
Would you please show me …	**Покажите мне, пожалуйста …** [paka'ʒite mne, pa'ʒaləstə …]
Would you please give me …	**Дайте мне, пожалуйста …** [dajte mne, pa'ʒaləstə …]
Can I try it on?	**Могу я это примерить?** [ma'gʊ ja 'ɛtə pri'meritʲ?]
Excuse me, where's the fitting room?	**Извините, где примерочная?** [izwi'nite, gde pri'merətʃnəja?]
Which color would you like?	**Какой цвет вы хотите?** [ka'kɔj tswet vɪ ha'tite?]
size	length	**размер	рост** [raz'mer	rɔst]
How does it fit?	**Подошло?** [pada'ʃlɔ?]
How much is it?	**Сколько это стоит?** ['skɔlʲkə 'ɛtə 'stoit?]
That's too expensive.	**Это слишком дорого.** ['ɛtə 'sliʃkəm 'dɔragə]
I'll take it.	**Я возьму это.** [ja vɔzʲ'mʊ 'ɛtə]
Excuse me, where do I pay?	**Извините, где касса?** [izwi'nite, gde 'kassa?]

Will you pay in cash or credit card?

Как вы будете платить?
[kak vɪ 'bʊdete pla'titʲ?]

In cash | with credit card

наличными | карточкой
[na'litʃnɪmi | 'kartətʃkəj]

Do you want the receipt?

Вам нужен чек?
[vam 'nʊʒən tʃek?]

Yes, please.

Да, будьте добры.
[da, 'butʲte dab'rɪ]

No, it's OK.

Нет, не надо. Спасибо.
[net, ne 'nadə. spa'sibə]

Thank you. Have a nice day!

Спасибо. Всего хорошего!
[spa'sibə. vse'vɔ ha'rɔʃəvə!]

In town

| Excuse me, please. | Извините, пожалуйста ...
[izwi'nite, pa'ʒaləstə ...] |
| I'm looking for ... | Я ищу ...
[ja i'ɕu ...] |

the subway	метро [me'trɔ]
my hotel	свою гостиницу [svɔ'ʝu gas'tinitsu]
the movie theater	кинотеатр [kinəte'atr]
a taxi stand	стоянку такси [sta'janku tak'si]

an ATM	банкомат [banka'mat]
a foreign exchange office	обмен валют [ab'men va'lʲut]
an internet café	интернет-кафе [intɛr'nɛt ka'fɛ]
... street	улицу ... [ulitsu ...]
this place	вот это место [vɔt 'ɛtə 'mestə]

| Do you know where ... is? | Вы не знаете, где находится ...?
[vɪ ne 'znaete, gde na'hɔditsa ...?] |
| Which street is this? | Как называется эта улица?
[kak nazɪ'vaetsa 'ɛta 'ulitsa?] |

Show me where we are right now.	Покажите, где мы сейчас. [paka'ʒite, gde mɪ se'tɕas]
Can I get there on foot?	Я дойду туда пешком? [ja daj'du tu'da peʃ'kɔm?]
Do you have a map of the city?	У вас есть карта города? [u vas estʲ 'karta 'gɔrada?]

How much is a ticket to get in?	Сколько стоит билет? ['skɔlʲkə 'stɔit bi'let?]
Can I take pictures here?	Здесь можно фотографировать? [zdesʲ 'mɔʒnə fɔtagra'firəvatʲ?]
Are you open?	Вы открыты? [vɪ atk'rɪtɪ?]

When do you open?

Во сколько вы открываетесь?
[vɔ 'skolʲkə vɪ atkrɪ'vaetesʲ?]

When do you close?

До которого часа вы работаете?
[dɔ ka'tɔrəvə 'tʃasa vɪ ra'bɔtaete?]

Money

money	**деньги** ['den^jgi]
cash	**наличные деньги** [na'litʃnɪe 'den^jgi]
paper money	**бумажные деньги** [bʊ'maʒnɪe 'den^jgi]
loose change	**мелочь** ['melotʃ]
check | change | tip	**счет | сдача | чаевые** [çʲot | 'sdatʃə | tʃəi'vɪe]
credit card	**кредитная карточка** [kre'ditnəja 'kartətʃka]
wallet	**бумажник** [bʊ'maʒnik]
to buy	**покупать** [pakʊ'patʲ]
to pay	**платить** [pla'titʲ]
fine	**штраф** [ʃtraf]
free	**бесплатно** [bisp'latnə]
Where can I buy ...?	**Где я могу купить ...?** [gde ja ma'gʊ kʊ'pitʲ ...?]
Is the bank open now?	**Банк сейчас открыт?** [bank se'tʃas atk'rɪt?]
When does it open?	**Во сколько он открывается?** [vɔ 'skolʲkə ɔn atkrɪ'vaetsa?]
When does it close?	**До которого часа он работает?** [dɔ ka'tɔrəvə 'tʃasa an ra'bɔtaet?]
How much?	**Сколько?** ['skolʲkə?]
How much is this?	**Сколько это стоит?** ['skolʲkə 'ɛtə 'stɔit?]
That's too expensive.	**Это слишком дорого.** ['ɛtə 'sliʃkəm 'dɔragə]
Excuse me, where do I pay?	**Извините, где касса?** [izwi'nite, gde 'kassa?]
Check, please.	**Счёт, пожалуйста.** [çʲot, pa'ʒaləstə]

Can I pay by credit card? | **Могу я заплатить карточкой?**
[ma'gʊ ja zapla'tit' 'kartətʃkəj?]

Is there an ATM here? | **Здесь есть банкомат?**
[zdesʲ estʲ banka'mat?]

I'm looking for an ATM. | **Мне нужен банкомат.**
[mne 'nʊʒən banka'mat]

I'm looking for a foreign exchange office. | **Я ищу обмен валют.**
[ja i'ɕu ab'men va'lʲʉt]

I'd like to change ... | **Я бы хотел /хотела/ поменять ...**
[ja bɪ ha'tel /ha'tela/ pame'ɲatʲ ...]

What is the exchange rate? | **Какой курс обмена?**
[ka'koj kʊrs ab'mena]

Do you need my passport? | **Вам нужен мой паспорт?**
[vam 'nʊʒən mɔj 'paspərt?]

Time

What time is it?	**Который час?** [ka'torɪj ʧas?]
When?	**Когда?** [kag'da?]
At what time?	**Во сколько?** [va 'skolʲkə?]
now	later	after ...	**сейчас	позже	после ...** [se'ʧas	'poʑʑe	'posle ...]
one o'clock	**Час дня** [ʧas dɲa]
one fifteen	**Час пятнадцать** [ʧas pit'natsatʲ]
one thirty	**Час тридцать** [ʧas t'rittsatʲ]
one forty-five	**Без пятнадцати два** [bez pit'natsati dva]
one	two	three	**один	два	три** [a'din	dva	tri]
four	five	six	**четыре	пять	шесть** [ʧe'tɪre	pʲatʲ	ʃestʲ]
seven	eight	nine	**семь	восемь	девять** [semʲ	'vosemʲ	'devʲatʲ]
ten	eleven	twelve	**десять	одиннадцать	двенадцать** ['desʲatʲ	a'dinnatsatʲ	dwi'natsatʲ]
in ...	**через ...** [ʧerez ...]
five minutes	**5 минут** [pʲatʲ mi'nut]
ten minutes	**10 минут** ['desʲatʲ mi'nut]
fifteen minutes	**15 минут** [pit'natsatʲ mi'nut]
twenty minutes	**20 минут** ['dvatsatʲ mi'nut]
half an hour	**полчаса** [polʧa'sa]
an hour	**один час** [a'din ʧas]

in the morning	**утром** ['utrəm]
early in the morning	**рано утром** [ranə 'utrəm]
this morning	**сегодня утром** [se'vodɲa 'utrəm]
tomorrow morning	**завтра утром** ['zaftrə 'utrəm]
at noon	**в обед** [v a'bet]
in the afternoon	**после обеда** ['pɔsle a'beda]
in the evening	**вечером** ['wetʃerəm]
tonight	**сегодня вечером** [se'vodɲa 'wetʃerəm]
at night	**ночью** ['nɔtʃʲʉ]
yesterday	**вчера** [vtʃe'ra]
today	**сегодня** [si'vodɲa]
tomorrow	**завтра** ['zaftra]
the day after tomorrow	**послезавтра** [pɔsle'zaftra]
What day is it today?	**Какой сегодня день?** [ka'kɔj si'vodɲa denʲ?]
It's …	**Сегодня …** [se'vodɲa …]
Monday	**понедельник** [pani'delʲnik]
Tuesday	**вторник** ['ftɔrnik]
Wednesday	**среда** [sri'da]
Thursday	**четверг** [tʃet'werk]
Friday	**пятница** ['pʲatnitsa]
Saturday	**суббота** [sʉ'bɔta]
Sunday	**воскресение** [vaskrə'seɲje]

Greetings. Introductions

Hello.
Здравствуйте.
['zdrastvujte]

Pleased to meet you.
Рад /рада/ с вами познакомиться.
[rad /'rada/ s 'vami pazna'komitsa]

Me too.
Я тоже.
[ja 'toʒɛ]

I'd like you to meet …
Знакомьтесь. Это …
[zna'komʲtesʲ. 'ɛtə …]

Nice to meet you.
Очень приятно.
[ɔtʃenʲ priˈjatnə]

How are you?
Как вы? | Как у вас дела?
[kak vɪ? | kak u vas de'la?]

My name is …
Меня зовут …
[mi'ɲa za'vut …]

His name is …
Его зовут …
[e'vɔ za'vut …]

Her name is …
Её зовут …
[eʲo za'vut …]

What's your name?
Как вас зовут?
[kak vas za'vut?]

What's his name?
Как его зовут?
[kak e'vɔ za'vut?]

What's her name?
Как ее зовут?
[kak eʲo za'vut?]

What's your last name?
Как ваша фамилия?
[kak 'vaʃʌ fa'milija?]

You can call me …
Зовите меня …
[za'wite me'ɲa …]

Where are you from?
Откуда вы?
[at'kuda vɪ]

I'm from …
Я из …
[ja iz …]

What do you do for a living?
Кем вы работаете?
[kem vɪ ra'botaete?]

Who is this?
Кто это?
[ktɔ 'ɛtə?]

Who is he?
Кто он?
[ktɔ ɔn?]

Who is she?
Кто она?
[ktɔ a'na?]

Who are they?
Кто они?
[ktɔ a'ni?]

This is …	Это …
	['ɛtə …]
my friend (masc.)	мой друг
	[mɔj drʊk]
my friend (fem.)	моя подруга
	[ma'ja pad'rʊga]
my husband	мой муж
	[mɔj mʊʃ]
my wife	моя жена
	[ma'ja ʒi'na]

my father	мой отец
	[mɔj a'tets]
my mother	моя мама
	[ma'ja 'mama]
my brother	мой брат
	[mɔj brat]
my sister	моя сестра
	[ma'ja sist'ra]
my son	мой сын
	[mɔj sɪn]
my daughter	моя дочь
	[ma'ja dɔtʃʲ]

This is our son.	Это наш сын.
	['ɛtə naʃ sɪn]
This is our daughter.	Это наша дочь.
	['ɛtə 'naʃʌ dɔtʃʲ]
These are my children.	Это мои дети.
	['ɛtə ma'i 'deti]
These are our children.	Это наши дети.
	['ɛtə 'naʃi 'deti]

Farewells

Good bye!	До свидания! [do swi'danija!]
Bye! (inform.)	Пока! [pa'ka!]
See you tomorrow.	До завтра. [do 'zaftra]
See you soon.	До встречи. [do vstr'etʃi]
See you at seven.	Встретимся в семь. [vstr'etimsʲa v semʲ]
Have fun!	Развлекайтесь! [razvle'kajtesʲ!]
Talk to you later.	Поговорим попозже. [pagava'rim pa'pozzə]
Have a nice weekend.	Удачных выходных. [u'datʃnıh vıhad'nıh]
Good night.	Спокойной ночи. [spa'kojnəj 'notʃi]
It's time for me to go.	Мне пора. [mne pa'ra]
I have to go.	Мне надо идти. [mne 'nadə it'ti]
I will be right back.	Я сейчас вернусь. [ja se'tʃas wer'nusʲ]
It's late.	Уже поздно. [u'ʒɛ 'pozdnə]
I have to get up early.	Мне рано вставать. [mne 'ranə vsta'vatʲ]
I'm leaving tomorrow.	Я завтра уезжаю. [ja 'zaftra ue'zzaʲu]
We're leaving tomorrow.	Мы завтра уезжаем. [mı 'zaftra ue'zzaem]
Have a nice trip!	Счастливой поездки! [ɕas'livəj pa'eztki!]
It was nice meeting you.	Было приятно с вами познакомиться. ['bılə pri'jatnə s 'vami pazna'komitsa]
It was nice talking to you.	Было приятно с вами пообщаться. ['bılə pri'jatnə s 'vami paab'ɕatsa]

Thanks for everything.	**Спасибо за всё.** [spa'sibə za 'vsʲo]
I had a very good time.	**Я прекрасно провёл /провела/ время.** [ja pre'krasnə pra'wʲol /prawe'la/ 'vremʲa]
We had a very good time.	**Мы прекрасно провели время.** [mɪ pre'krasnə prawe'li 'vremʲa]
It was really great.	**Всё было замечательно.** [vsʲo 'bɪlə zame'ʧʲatelʲnə]
I'm going to miss you.	**Я буду скучать.** [ja 'bʊdʊ skʊ'ʧʲatʲ]
We're going to miss you.	**Мы будем скучать.** [mɪ 'bʊdem skʊ'ʧʲatʲ]
Good luck!	**Удачи! Счастливо!** [u'daʧʲi! 'ɕaslivə!]
Say hi to …	**Передавайте привет …** [pereda'vajte pri'wet …]

Foreign language

I don't understand.	**Я не понимаю.** [ja ne pani'maʲʉ]
Write it down, please.	**Напишите это, пожалуйста.** [napi'ʃite 'ɛtə, pa'ʒaləstə]
Do you speak …?	**Вы знаете …?** [vɪ 'znaete …?]

I speak a little bit of …	**Я немного знаю …** [ja nem'nɔgə 'znaʲʉ …]
English	**английский** [ang'lijskij]
Turkish	**турецкий** [tʉ'reʦkij]
Arabic	**арабский** [a'rapskij]
French	**французский** [fran'ʦuskij]

German	**немецкий** [ne'meʦkij]
Italian	**итальянский** [ita'ljanskij]
Spanish	**испанский** [is'panskij]
Portuguese	**португальский** [partʉgalʲskij]
Chinese	**китайский** [ki'tajskij]
Japanese	**японский** [ja'pɔnskij]

Can you repeat that, please.	**Повторите, пожалуйста.** [pavta'rite, pa'ʒaləstə]
I understand.	**Я понимаю.** [ja pani'maʲʉ]
I don't understand.	**Я не понимаю.** [ja ne pani'maʲʉ]
Please speak more slowly.	**Говорите медленнее, пожалуйста.** [gava'rite 'medlenee, pa'ʒaləstə]

Is that correct? (Am I saying it right?)	**Это правильно?** ['ɛtə 'prawilʲnə?]
What is this? (What does this mean?)	**Что это?** [ʃtɔ 'ɛtə?]

Apologies

Excuse me, please.
Извините, пожалуйста.
[izwi'nite, pa'ʒaləstə]

I'm sorry.
Я сожалею.
[ja saʒə'leʲʉ]

I'm really sorry.
Мне очень жаль.
[mne 'otʃenʲ ʒalʲ]

Sorry, it's my fault.
Виноват /Виновата/, это моя вина.
[wina'vat /wina'vata/, 'ɛtə ma'ja wi'na]

My mistake.
Моя ошибка.
[ma'ja a'ʃipka]

May I ...?
Могу я ...?
[ma'gʊ ja ...?]

Do you mind if I ...?
Вы не будете возражать, если я ...?
[vɪ ne 'bʊdete vazra'ʒatʲ, 'esli ja ...?]

It's OK.
Ничего страшного.
[nitʃe'vɔ 'straʃnəvə]

It's all right.
Всё в порядке.
[vsʲo v pa'rʲatke]

Don't worry about it.
Не беспокойтесь.
[ne bespa'kɔjtesʲ]

Agreement

Yes.	**Да.** [da]
Yes, sure.	**Да, конечно.** [da, ka'neʃnə]
OK (Good!)	**Хорошо!** [hara'ʃɔ!]
Very well.	**Очень хорошо.** ['ɔtʃenʲ hara'ʃɔ]
Certainly!	**Конечно!** [ka'neʃnə!]
I agree.	**Я согласен /согласна/.** [ja sag'lasen /sag'lasna/]
That's correct.	**Верно.** ['wernə]
That's right.	**Правильно.** ['prawilʲnə]
You're right.	**Вы правы.** [vɪ 'pravɪ]
I don't mind.	**Я не возражаю.** [ja ne vazra'ʒaʲʉ]
Absolutely right.	**Совершенно верно.** [sawer'ʃɛnnə 'wernə]
It's possible.	**Это возможно.** ['ɛtə vaz'mɔʒnə]
That's a good idea.	**Это хорошая мысль.** [ɛtə ha'rɔʃəja mɪslʲ]
I can't say no.	**Не могу отказать.** [ne ma'gʊ atka'zatʲ]
I'd be happy to.	**Буду рад /рада/.** [bʊdʊ rad /'rada/]
With pleasure.	**С удовольствием.** [s uda'vɔlʲstwiem]

Refusal. Expressing doubt

No.	**Нет.**
	[net]
Certainly not.	**Конечно нет.**
	[ka'neʃnə net]
I don't agree.	**Я не согласен /не согласна/.**
	[ja ne sag'lasen /ne sag'lasna/]
I don't think so.	**Я так не думаю.**
	[ja tak ne 'dumaʲʉ]
It's not true.	**Это неправда.**
	['ɛtə nep'ravda]
You are wrong.	**Вы неправы.**
	[vɪ nep'ravɪ]
I think you are wrong.	**Я думаю, что вы неправы.**
	[ja 'dumaʲʉ, ʃtɔ vɪ nep'ravɪ]
I'm not sure.	**Не уверен /не уверена/.**
	[ne u'veren /ne u'verena/]
It's impossible.	**Это невозможно.**
	['ɛtə nevaz'mɔʒnə]
Nothing of the kind (sort)!	**Ничего подобного!**
	[niʧe'vɔ pa'dɔbnevə!]
The exact opposite.	**Наоборот!**
	[naaba'rɔt!]
I'm against it.	**Я против.**
	[ja 'prɔtiv]
I don't care.	**Мне всё равно.**
	[mne vsʲo rav'nɔ]
I have no idea.	**Понятия не имею.**
	[pa'ɲatija ne i'meʲʉ]
I doubt that.	**Сомневаюсь, что это так.**
	[samne'vaʲʉsʲ, ʃtɔ 'ɛtə tak]
Sorry, I can't.	**Извините, я не могу.**
	[izwi'nite, ja ne ma'gu]
Sorry, I don't want to.	**Извините, я не хочу.**
	[izwi'nite, ja ne ha'ʧu]
Thank you, but I don't need this.	**Спасибо, мне это не нужно.**
	[spa'sibə, mne 'ɛtə ne 'nuʒnə]
It's late.	**Уже поздно.**
	[u'ʒɛ 'pɔzdnə]

I have to get up early.

Мне рано вставать.
[mne 'ranə vsta'vatʲ]

I don't feel well.

Я плохо себя чувствую.
[ja 'plɔhə se'bʲa 'tʃustvuʲu]

Expressing gratitude

Thank you.	**Спасибо.** [spa'sibə]
Thank you very much.	**Спасибо большое.** [spa'sibə bal^j'ʃoe]
I really appreciate it.	**Очень признателен /признательна/.** [ɔʧen^j priz'natelen /priz'natel^jna/]
I'm really grateful to you.	**Я вам благодарен /благодарна/.** [ja vam blaga'daren /blaga'darna/]
We are really grateful to you.	**Мы Вам благодарны.** [mɪ vam blaga'darnɪ]

Thank you for your time.	**Спасибо, что потратили время.** [spa'sibə, ʃtɔ pat'ratili 'vrem^ja]
Thanks for everything.	**Спасибо за всё.** [spa'sibə za 'vs^jo]
Thank you for ...	**Спасибо за ...** [spa'sibə za ...]
your help	**вашу помощь** [vaʃʋ 'pomaɕ]
a nice time	**хорошее время** [ha'roʃee 'vrem^ja]

a wonderful meal	**прекрасную еду** [pre'krasnʋʉ e'dʋ]
a pleasant evening	**приятный вечер** [pri'jatnɪj 'weʧer]
a wonderful day	**замечательный день** [zami'ʧatel^jnɪj den^j]
an amazing journey	**интересную экскурсию** [inte'resnʋʉ ɛks'kʋrsi^jʉ]

Don't mention it.	**Не за что.** [ne za ʃtə]
You are welcome.	**Не стоит благодарности.** [ne 'stɔit blaga'darnasti]
Any time.	**Всегда пожалуйста.** [vseg'da pa'ʒaləsta]
My pleasure.	**Был рад /Была рада/ помочь.** [bɪl rad /bɪ'la 'rada/ pa'moʧ]
Forget it. It's alright.	**Забудьте. Всё в порядке.** [za'bʋt^jte. fs^jo f po'r^jatke]
Don't worry about it.	**Не беспокойтесь.** [ne bespa'kɔjtes^j]

Congratulations. Best wishes

Congratulations!	**Поздравляю!** [pazdrav'ʎaʲʉ!]
Happy birthday!	**С днём рождения!** [s 'dnʲom raʒ'denija!]
Merry Christmas!	**Весёлого рождества!** [we'sʲoləvə raʒdest'va!]
Happy New Year!	**С Новым годом!** [s 'nɔvɪm 'gɔdəm!]

Happy Easter!	**Со Светлой Пасхой!** [sɔ 'swetləj 'pashəj!]
Happy Hanukkah!	**Счастливой Хануки!** [ɕas'livəj 'hanʊki!]

I'd like to propose a toast.	**У меня есть тост.** [u me'ɲa estʲ tɔst]
Cheers!	**За ваше здоровье!** [za 'vaʃə zda'rɔvje]
Let's drink to ...!	**Выпьем за ... !** ['vɪpjem za ... !]
To our success!	**За наш успех!** [za naʃ us'peh!]
To your success!	**За ваш успех!** [za vaʃ us'peh!]

Good luck!	**Удачи!** [u'datɕi!]
Have a nice day!	**Приятного вам дня!** [pri'jatnəvə vam dɲa!]
Have a good holiday!	**Хорошего вам отдыха!** [ha'rɔʃevə vam 'ɔtdɪha!]
Have a safe journey!	**Удачной поездки!** [u'datɕnəj pa'eztki!]
I hope you get better soon!	**Желаю вам скорого выздоровления!** [ʒe'laʲʉ vam 'skɔrəvə vɪzdarav'lenija!]

Socializing

Why are you sad?
Почему вы расстроены?
[pat͡ʃe'mʊ vɪ rast'rɔenɪ?]

Smile! Cheer up!
Улыбнитесь!
[ulɪb'nitesʲl]

Are you free tonight?
Вы не заняты сегодня вечером?
[vɪ ne zaɲatɪ se'vɔdɲa 'wet͡ʃerəm?]

May I offer you a drink?
Могу я предложить вам выпить?
[ma'gʊ ja predla'ʒitʲ vam 'vɪpitʲ?]

Would you like to dance?
Не хотите потанцевать?
[ne ha'tite patant͡se'vatʲ?]

Let's go to the movies.
Может сходим в кино?
['mɔʒet 'shɔdim v ki'nɔ?]

May I invite you to …?
Могу я пригласить вас в …?
[ma'gʊ ja prigla'sitʲ vas v …?]

a restaurant
ресторан
[resta'ran]

the movies
кино
[ki'nɔ]

the theater
театр
[te'atr]

go for a walk
на прогулку
[na pra'gʊlkʊ]

At what time?
Во сколько?
[va 'skɔlʲkə?]

tonight
сегодня вечером
[se'vɔdɲa 'wet͡ʃerəm]

at six
в 6 часов
[v ʃɛstʲ t͡ʃa'sɔf]

at seven
в 7 часов
[v semʲ t͡ʃa'sɔf]

at eight
в 8 часов
[v 'vɔsemʲ t͡ʃa'sɔf]

at nine
в 9 часов
[v 'devʲatʲ t͡ʃa'sɔf]

Do you like it here?
Вам здесь нравится?
[vam zdesʲ 'nrawit͡sa?]

Are you here with someone?
Вы здесь с кем-то?
[vɪ zdesʲ s 'kem tə?]

I'm with my friend.
Я с другом /подругой/.
[ja s 'drʊgəm /pad'rʊgəj/]

I'm with my friends.

Я с друзьями.
[ja s dru'zj'ami]

No, I'm alone.

Я один /одна/.
[ja a'din /ad'na/]

Do you have a boyfriend?

У тебя есть приятель?
[u te'b'a est' pri'jatel'?]

I have a boyfriend.

У меня есть друг.
[u me'na est' druk]

Do you have a girlfriend?

У тебя есть подружка?
[u te'b'a est' pad'ruʃka?]

I have a girlfriend.

У меня есть девушка.
[u me'na est' 'devuʃka]

Can I see you again?

Мы еще встретимся?
[mɪ e'ɕo vst'retims'a?]

Can I call you?

Можно я тебе позвоню?
[moʒnə ja te'be pazva'n'u?]

Call me. (Give me a call.)

Позвони мне.
[pazva'ni mne]

What's your number?

Какой у тебя номер?
[ka'koj u te'b'a 'nomer?]

I miss you.

Я скучаю по тебе.
[ja sku'tʃa'u pa te'be]

You have a beautiful name.

У вас очень красивое имя.
[u vas 'otʃen' kra'sivae 'im'a]

I love you.

Я тебя люблю.
[ja te'b'a l'ub'l'u]

Will you marry me?

Выходи за меня.
[vɪha'di za me'na]

You're kidding!

Вы шутите!
[vɪ 'ʃutite!]

I'm just kidding.

Я просто шучу.
[ja 'prostə ʃu'tʃu]

Are you serious?

Вы серьезно?
[vɪ se'rjoznə?]

I'm serious.

Я серьёзно.
[ja se'rj'oznə]

Really?!

Правда?!
['pravda?!]

It's unbelievable!

Это невероятно!
['ɛtə newera'jatnə]

I don't believe you.

Я вам не верю.
[ja vam ne 'wer'u]

I can't.

Я не могу.
[ja ne ma'gu]

I don't know.

Я не знаю.
[ja ne 'zna'u]

I don't understand you.

Я вас не понимаю.
[ja vas ne pani'ma'u]

Please go away.

Уйдите, пожалуйста.
[uj'dite, pa'ʒaləstə]

Leave me alone!

Оставьте меня в покое!
[as'tavʲte meˈɲa v paˈkɔe!]

I can't stand him.

Я его не выношу.
[ja eˈgɔ ne vɪnaˈʃʊ]

You are disgusting!

Вы отвратительны!
[vɪ atvraˈtitelʲnɪ!]

I'll call the police!

Я вызову полицию!
[ja ˈvɪzavʊ paˈlitsɪʲʉ!]

Sharing impressions. Emotions

I like it.	Мне это нравится. [mne 'ɛtə 'nrawiʦa]
Very nice.	Очень мило. ['ɔʧenʲ 'milə]
That's great!	Это здорово! ['ɛtə 'zdɔrəvə!]
It's not bad.	Это неплохо. ['ɛtə nep'lɔhə]

I don't like it.	Мне это не нравится. [mne 'ɛtə ne 'nrawiʦa]
It's not good.	Это нехорошо. ['ɛtə nehara'ʃo]
It's bad.	Это плохо. ['ɛtə 'plɔhə]
It's very bad.	Это очень плохо. ['ɛtə 'ɔʧenʲ 'plɔhə]
It's disgusting.	Это отвратительно. ['ɛtə atvra'titelʲnə]

I'm happy.	Я счастлив /счастлива/. [ja 'ɕasliv /'ɕasliva/]
I'm content.	Я доволен /довольна/. [ja da'vɔlen /da'vɔlʲna/]
I'm in love.	Я влюблён /влюблена/. [ja vlʲub'lʲon /vlʲuble'na/]
I'm calm.	Я спокоен /спокойна/. [ja spa'kɔen /spa'kɔjna/]
I'm bored.	Мне скучно. [mne 'skuʃnə]

I'm tired.	Я устал /устала/. [ja us'tal /us'tala/]
I'm sad.	Мне грустно. [mne 'grusnə]
I'm frightened.	Я напуган /напугана/. [ja na'pugan /na'pugana/]

I'm angry.	Я злюсь. [ja zlʲusʲ]
I'm worried.	Я волнуюсь. [ja val'nuʲusʲ]
I'm nervous.	Я нервничаю. [ja 'nervniʧaʲu]

I'm jealous. (envious)	**Я завидую.** [ja zaˈwiduʲʉ]
I'm surprised.	**Я удивлён /удивлена/.** [ja udivˈlʲon /udivleˈna/]
I'm perplexed.	**Я озадачен /озадачена/.** [ja azaˈdatʃen /azaˈdatʃena/]

Problems. Accidents

I've got a problem.
У меня проблема.
[u me'ɲa prab'lema]

We've got a problem.
У нас проблема.
[u nas prab'lema]

I'm lost.
Я заблудился /заблудилась/.
[ja zablu'dilsʲa /zablu'dilasʲ/]

I missed the last bus (train).
Я опоздал на последний автобус (поезд).
[ja apaz'dal na pas'lednij aft'ɔbus ('pɔest)]

I don't have any money left.
У меня совсем не осталось денег.
[u me'ɲa sav'sem ne as'taləsʲ 'denek]

I've lost my ...
Я потерял /потеряла/ ...
[ja pate'rʲal /pate'rʲala/ ...]

Someone stole my ...
У меня украли ...
[u me'ɲa uk'rali ...]

passport
паспорт
['paspərt]

wallet
бумажник
[bu'maʒnik]

papers
документы
[daku'mentɪ]

ticket
билет
[bi'let]

money
деньги
['denʲgi]

handbag
сумку
['sumku]

camera
фотоаппарат
['fota apa'rat]

laptop
ноутбук
[nɔut'buk]

tablet computer
планшет
[plan'ʃət]

mobile phone
телефон
[tele'fɔn]

Help me!
Помогите!
[pama'gite]

What's happened?
Что случилось?
[ʃtɔ slu'tʃiləsʲ?]

fire	**пожар** [pa'ʒar]
shooting	**стрельба** [strelʲ'ba]
murder	**убийство** [u'bijstvə]
explosion	**взрыв** [vzrɪv]
fight	**драка** ['draka]

Call the police!	**Вызовите полицию!** ['vɪzawite pa'litsɨʲʉ!]
Please hurry up!	**Пожалуйста, быстрее!** [pa'ʒaləstə, bɪst'ree!]
I'm looking for the police station.	**Я ищу полицейский участок.** [ja i'ɕu pali'tsɛjskij u'tʃastək]
I need to make a call.	**Мне нужно позвонить.** [mne 'nuʒnə pazva'nitʲ]
May I use your phone?	**Могу я позвонить?** [ma'gu ja pazva'nitʲ?]

I've been …	**Меня …** [mi'na …]
mugged	**ограбили** [ag'rabili]
robbed	**обокрали** [abak'rali]
raped	**изнасиловали** [izna'siləvali]
attacked (beaten up)	**избили** [iz'bili]

Are you all right?	**С вами все в порядке?** [s 'vami vsʲo v pa'rʲatke?]
Did you see who it was?	**Вы видели, кто это был?** [vɪ 'wideli, ktɔ 'ɛtə bɪl?]
Would you be able to recognize the person?	**Вы сможете его узнать?** [vɪ s'mɔʒete e'vɔ uz'natʲ?]
Are you sure?	**Вы точно уверены?** [vɪ 'tɔtʃnə u'werenɪ?]

Please calm down.	**Пожалуйста, успокойтесь.** [pa'ʒaləstə, uspa'kojtesʲ]
Take it easy!	**Спокойнее!** [spa'kojnee!]
Don't worry!	**Не беспокойтесь.** [ne bespa'kojtesʲ]
Everything will be fine.	**Всё будет хорошо.** [vsʲo 'bʊdet hara'ʃɔ]
Everything's all right.	**Всё в порядке.** [vsʲo v pa'rʲatke]

Come here, please.	**Подойдите, пожалуйста.** [padaj'dite, pa'ʒaləstə]
I have some questions for you.	**У меня к вам несколько вопросов.** [u me'ɲa k vam 'neskalʲkə vap'rɔsəf]
Wait a moment, please.	**Подождите, пожалуйста.** [padaʒ'dite, pa'ʒaləstə]
Do you have any I.D.?	**У вас есть документы?** [u vas estʲ daku'mentɪ?]
Thanks. You can leave now.	**Спасибо. Вы можете идти.** [spa'sibə. vɪ 'mɔʒɛte it'ti]
Hands behind your head!	**Руки за голову!** ['ruki 'zagalavʊ!]
You're under arrest!	**Вы арестованы!** [vɪ ares'tɔvanɪ!]

Health problems

Please help me.	**Помогите, пожалуйста.** [pama'gite, pa'ʒalestə]
I don't feel well.	**Мне плохо.** [mne 'pləhə]
My husband doesn't feel well.	**Моему мужу плохо.** [mae'mʊ 'mʊʒu 'pləhə]
My son ...	**Моему сыну ...** [mae'mʊ 'sɪnʊ ...]
My father ...	**Моему отцу ...** [mae'mʊ at'tsu ...]
My wife doesn't feel well.	**Моей жене плохо.** [ma'ej ʒɛne 'pləhə]
My daughter ...	**Моей дочери ...** [ma'ej 'dɔtʃeri ...]
My mother ...	**Моей матери ...** [ma'ej 'materi ...]
I've got a ...	**У меня болит ...** [u me'ɲa ba'lit ...]
headache	**голова** [gala'va]
sore throat	**горло** ['gorlə]
stomach ache	**живот** [ʒɪ'vɔt]
toothache	**зуб** [zup]
I feel dizzy.	**У меня кружится голова.** [u me'ɲa krʊʒɪtsa gala'va]
He has a fever.	**У него температура.** [u ne'vɔ tempera'tʊra]
She has a fever.	**У неё температура.** [u ne'o tempera'tʊra]
I can't breathe.	**Я не могу дышать.** [ja ne ma'gʊ dɪ'ʃatʲ]
I'm short of breath.	**Я задыхаюсь.** [ja zadɪ'haʲʊsʲ]
I am asthmatic.	**Я астматик.** [ja ast'matik]
I am diabetic.	**Я диабетик.** [ja dia'betik]

I can't sleep.

У меня бессонница.
[u me'ɲa bes'sɔnitsa]

food poisoning

пищевое отравление
[piɕe'vɔe atrav'lenie]

It hurts here.

Болит вот здесь.
[ba'lit vɔt zdesʲ]

Help me!

Помогите!
[pama'gite!]

I am here!

Я здесь!
[ja zdesʲ!]

We are here!

Мы здесь!
[mɪ zdesʲ!]

Get me out of here!

Вытащите меня!
['vɪtaɕite me'ɲa!]

I need a doctor.

Мне нужен врач.
[mne 'nuʒən vratʃ]

I can't move.

Я не могу двигаться.
[ja ne ma'gu 'dvigatsa]

I can't move my legs.

Я не чувствую ног.
[ja ne 'tʃustvuʲu nɔk]

I have a wound.

Я ранен /ранена/.
[ja 'ranen /'ranena/]

Is it serious?

Это серьезно?
['ɛtə se'rʲʲoznə?]

My documents are in my pocket.

Мои документы в кармане.
[ma'i daku'mentɪ v kar'mane]

Calm down!

Успокойтесь!
[uspa'kɔjtesʲ!]

May I use your phone?

Могу я позвонить?
[ma'gu ja pazva'nitʲ?]

Call an ambulance!

Вызовите скорую!
[vɪzawite 'skɔruʲu!]

It's urgent!

Это срочно!
['ɛtə 'srɔtʃnə!]

It's an emergency!

Это очень срочно!
['ɛtə 'ɔtʃenʲ 'srɔtʃnə!]

Please hurry up!

Пожалуйста, быстрее!
[pa'ʒaləstə, bɪst'ree!]

Would you please call a doctor?

Вызовите врача, пожалуйста.
[vɪzawite vra'tʃa, pa'ʒaləstə]

Where is the hospital?

Скажите, где больница?
[ska'ʒite, gde balʲ'nitsa?]

How are you feeling?

Как вы себя чувствуете?
[kak vɪ se'bʲa 'tʃustvuete?]

Are you all right?

С вами все в порядке?
[s 'vami vsʲo v pa'rʲatke?]

What's happened?

Что случилось?
[ʃtɔ slu'tʃiləsʲ?]

I feel better now.	**Мне уже лучше.**
	[mne u'ʒe 'lutʃɛ]
It's OK.	**Всё в порядке.**
	[vsʲo v pa'rʲatke]
It's all right.	**Всё хорошо.**
	[vsʲo hara'ʃo]

At the pharmacy

pharmacy (drugstore)	**Аптека** [ap'teka]
24-hour pharmacy	**круглосуточная аптека** [krʊgla'sʊtətʃnəja ap'teka]
Where is the closest pharmacy?	**Где ближайшая аптека?** [gde blʲi'ʒajʃəja ap'teka?]
Is it open now?	**Она сейчас открыта?** [a'na se'tʃas atk'rɪta?]
At what time does it open?	**Во сколько она открывается?** [va 'skolʲkə a'na atkrɪ'vaeʦa?]
At what time does it close?	**До которого часа она работает?** [dɔ ka'tɔrəvə 'tʃasa a'na ra'bɔtaet?]
Is it far?	**Это далеко?** ['ɛtə dale'kɔ?]
Can I get there on foot?	**Я дойду туда пешком?** [ja daj'dʊ tʊ'da peʃ'kɔm?]
Can you show me on the map?	**Покажите мне на карте, пожалуйста.** [paka'ʒite mne na 'karte, pa'ʒaləstə]
Please give me something for ...	**Дайте мне, что-нибудь от ...** ['dajte mne, ʃtɔ nʲi'bʊtʲ ɔt ...]
a headache	**головной боли** [galav'nɔj 'bɔli]
a cough	**кашля** ['kaʃʎa]
a cold	**простуды** [pras'tʊdɪ]
the flu	**гриппа** ['gripa]
a fever	**температуры** [tempera'tʊrɪ]
a stomach ache	**боли в желудке** ['bɔli v ʒi'lutke]
nausea	**тошноты** [taʃna'tɪ]
diarrhea	**диареи** [dia'rei]
constipation	**запора** [za'pɔra]
pain in the back	**боль в спине** [bɔlʲ v spi'ne]

chest pain	**боль в груди** ['bɔlʲ v gru'di]
side stitch	**боль в боку** [bɔlʲ v ba'ku]
abdominal pain	**боль в животе** ['bɔlʲ v ʒiva'te]

pill	**таблетка** [tab'letka]
ointment, cream	**мазь, крем** [mazʲ, krem]
syrup	**сироп** [si'rɔp]
spray	**спрей** [sprɛj]
drops	**капли** ['kapli]

You need to go to the hospital.	**Вам нужно в больницу.** [vam 'nuʒnə v balʲ'nitsu]
health insurance	**страховка** [stra'hɔvka]
prescription	**рецепт** [re'tsept]
insect repellant	**средство от насекомых** ['sredstvə at nase'kɔmɪh]
Band Aid	**лейкопластырь** [lejkə'plastɪrʲ]

The bare minimum

Excuse me, ...	**Извините, ...** [izwi'nite, ...]
Hello.	**Здравствуйте.** ['zdrastvujte]
Thank you.	**Спасибо.** [spa'sibə]
Good bye.	**До свидания.** [da swi'danija]
Yes.	**Да.** [da]
No.	**Нет.** [net]
I don't know.	**Я не знаю.** [ja ne 'znaʲʊ]
Where? | Where to? | When?	**Где? | Куда? | Когда?** [gde? | kʊ'da? | kag'da?]

I need ...	**Мне нужен ...** [mne 'nʊʒən ...]
I want ...	**Я хочу ...** [ja ha'tʃu ...]
Do you have ...?	**У вас есть ...?** [u vas estʲ ...?]
Is there a ... here?	**Здесь есть ...?** [zdesʲ estʲ ...?]
May I ...?	**Я могу ...?** [ja ma'gʊ ...?]
..., please (polite request)	**пожалуйста** [pa'ʒaləstə]

I'm looking for ...	**Я ищу ...** [ja i'ɕu ...]
restroom	**туалет** [tʊa'let]
ATM	**банкомат** [banka'mat]
pharmacy (drugstore)	**аптеку** [ap'tekʊ]
hospital	**больницу** [balʲ'nitsu]
police station	**полицейский участок** [pali'tsɛjskij u'tʃastək]
subway	**метро** [met'rɔ]

taxi	**такси** [tak'si]
train station	**вокзал** [vak'zal]

My name is ...	**Меня зовут ...** [mi'ɲa za'vʊt ...]
What's your name?	**Как вас зовут?** [kak vas za'vʊt?]
Could you please help me?	**Помогите мне, пожалуйста.** [pama'gite mne, pa'ʒaləstə]
I've got a problem.	**У меня проблема.** [u me'ɲa prab'lema]
I don't feel well.	**Мне плохо.** [mne 'pləhə]
Call an ambulance!	**Вызовите скорую!** [vɪzawite 'skorʊʲʊ!]
May I make a call?	**Могу я позвонить?** [ma'gʊ ja pazva'nitʲ?]

I'm sorry.	**Извините.** [izwi'nite]
You're welcome.	**Пожалуйста.** [pa'ʒaləstə]

I, me	**я** [ja]
you (inform.)	**ты** [tɪ]
he	**он** [ɔn]
she	**она** [a'na]
they (masc.)	**они** [a'ni]
they (fem.)	**они** [a'ni]
we	**мы** [mɪ]
you (pl)	**вы** [vɪ]
you (sg, form.)	**Вы** [vɪ]

ENTRANCE	**ВХОД** [vhɔt]
EXIT	**ВЫХОД** ['vɪhət]
OUT OF ORDER	**НЕ РАБОТАЕТ** [ne ra'botaet]
CLOSED	**ЗАКРЫТО** [zak'rɪtə]

OPEN

ОТКРЫТО
[atk'rɪtə]

FOR WOMEN

ДЛЯ ЖЕНЩИН
[dʌa 'ʒɛnɕin]

FOR MEN

ДЛЯ МУЖЧИН
[dʌa mʊ'ɕin]

MINI DICTIONARY

This section contains 250 useful words required for everyday communication. You will find the names of months and days of the week here. The dictionary also contains topics such as colors, measurements, family, and more

T&P Books Publishing

DICTIONARY CONTENTS

T&P Books Publishing

1. Time. Calendar

time	время (с)	[v'rem^ja]

time	время (с)	[v'remʲa]
hour	час (м)	[t͡ʃas]
half an hour	полчаса (мн)	[palt͡ʃe'sa]
minute	минута (ж)	[mi'nʊtə]
second	секунда (ж)	[si'kʊndə]

today (adv)	сегодня	[si'vɔdɲa]
tomorrow (adv)	завтра	['zaftrə]
yesterday (adv)	вчера	[ft͡ʃi'ra]

Monday	понедельник (м)	[pani'deʌnik]
Tuesday	вторник (м)	[f'tɔrnik]
Wednesday	среда (ж)	[sre'da]
Thursday	четверг (м)	[t͡ʃit'werk]
Friday	пятница (ж)	['pʲatnit͡sə]
Saturday	суббота (ж)	[sʊ'bɔtə]
Sunday	воскресенье (с)	[vaskri'seɲje]

day	день (м)	[deɲ]
working day	рабочий день (м)	[ra'bɔt͡ʃij deɲ]
public holiday	празник (м)	[p'raznik]
weekend	выходные (мн)	[vɪhad'nɪe]

week	неделя (ж)	[ni'deʌa]
last week (adv)	на прошлой неделе	[na p'rɔʃlaj ni'dele]
next week (adv)	на следующей неделе	[na sle'dʊɕej ni'dele]

| in the morning | утром | ['utram] |
| in the afternoon | после обеда | ['pɔsle a'bedə] |

| in the evening | вечером | ['wet͡ʃeram] |
| tonight (this evening) | сегодня вечером | [si'vɔdɲa 'wet͡ʃeram] |

| at night | ночью | ['nɔt͡ʃy] |
| midnight | полночь (ж) | ['pɔlnat͡ʃ] |

January	январь (м)	[en'varʲ]
February	февраль (м)	[fiv'raʌ]
March	март (м)	[mart]
April	апрель (м)	[ap'reʌ]
May	май (м)	[maj]
June	июнь (м)	[i'juɲ]

| July | июль (м) | [i'juʌ] |
| August | август (м) | ['avgʊst] |

September	сентябрь (м)	[sin'tʲabrʲ]
October	октябрь (м)	[ak'tʲabrʲ]
November	ноябрь (м)	[na'jabrʲ]
December	декабрь (м)	[di'kabrʲ]

in spring	весной	[wis'nɔj]
in summer	летом	['letam]
in fall	осенью	['ɔseɲy]
in winter	зимой	[zi'mɔj]

month	месяц (м)	['mesit͡s]
season (summer, etc.)	сезон (м)	[si'zɔn]
year	год (м)	[gɔt]

2. Numbers. Numerals

0 zero	ноль	[nɔʎ]
1 one	один	[a'din]
2 two	два	[dvə]
3 three	три	[tri]
4 four	четыре	[t͡ʃi'tɪre]

5 five	пять	[pʲatʲ]
6 six	шесть	[ʃestʲ]
7 seven	семь	[semʲ]
8 eight	восемь	['vɔsemʲ]
9 nine	девять	['dewitʲ]
10 ten	десять	['desitʲ]

11 eleven	одиннадцать	[a'dinat͡satʲ]
12 twelve	двенадцать	[dwi'nat͡satʲ]
13 thirteen	тринадцать	[tri'nat͡satʲ]
14 fourteen	четырнадцать	[t͡ʃi'tɪrnat͡satʲ]
15 fifteen	пятнадцать	[pit'nat͡satʲ]

16 sixteen	шестнадцать	[ʃɛs'nat͡satʲ]
17 seventeen	семнадцать	[sim'nat͡satʲ]
18 eighteen	восемнадцать	[vasem'nat͡satʲ]
19 nineteen	девятнадцать	[diwit'nat͡satʲ]

20 twenty	двадцать	[d'vat͡satʲ]
30 thirty	тридцать	[t'rit͡satʲ]
40 forty	сорок	['sɔrak]
50 fifty	пятьдесят	[pitʲdi'sʲat]

60 sixty	шестьдесят	[ʃistʲdi'sʲat]
70 seventy	семьдесят	['semʲdisit]
80 eighty	восемьдесят	['vɔsemʲdisit]
90 ninety	девяносто	[diwi'nɔstə]
100 one hundred	сто	[stɔ]

200 two hundred	двести	[d'westi]
300 three hundred	триста	[t'ristə]
400 four hundred	четыреста	[tʃi'tɪrestə]
500 five hundred	пятьсот	[pi'tsɔt]

600 six hundred	шестьсот	[ʃɛs'sɔt]
700 seven hundred	семьсот	[simʲ'sɔt]
800 eight hundred	восемьсот	[vasemʲ'sɔt]
900 nine hundred	девятьсот	[diwi'tsɔt]
1000 one thousand	тысяча	['tɪsitʃə]

| 10000 ten thousand | десять тысяч | ['desitʲ 'tɪsitʃ] |
| one hundred thousand | сто тысяч | [stɔ 'tɪsitʃ] |

| million | миллион (м) | [mili'ɔn] |
| billion | миллиард (м) | [mili'art] |

3. Humans. Family

man (adult male)	мужчина (м)	[mʊ'ɕinə]
young man	юноша (м)	['junaʃə]
woman	женщина (ж)	['ʒɛɲɕinə]
girl (young woman)	девушка (ж)	['devʊʃkə]
old man	старик (м)	[sta'rik]
old woman	старая женщина (м)	[s'tarajə 'ʒɛɲɕinə]

mother	мать (ж)	[matʲ]
father	отец (м)	[a'teʦ]
son	сын (м)	[sɪn]
daughter	дочь (ж)	[dotʃ]
brother	брат (м)	[brat]
sister	сестра (ж)	[sist'ra]

parents	родители (мн)	[ra'diteli]
child	ребёнок (м)	[ri'bɜnak]
children	дети (мн)	['deti]
stepmother	мачеха (ж)	['matʃehə]
stepfather	отчим (м)	['otʃim]

grandmother	бабушка (ж)	['babʊʃkə]
grandfather	дедушка (м)	['dedʊʃkə]
grandson	внук (м)	[vnʊk]
granddaughter	внучка (ж)	[v'nutʃkə]
grandchildren	внуки (мн)	[v'nʊki]

uncle	дядя (м)	['dʲadʲa]
aunt	тётя (ж)	['tɜtʲa]
nephew	племянник (м)	[pli'mʲanik]
niece	племянница (ж)	[pli'mʲanitsə]
wife	жена (ж)	[ʒɪ'na]

husband	муж (м)	[muʃ]
married (masc.)	женатый	[ʒɪˈnatɪj]
married (fem.)	замужняя	[zaˈmuʒnija]
widow	вдова (ж)	[vdaˈva]
widower	вдовец (м)	[vdaˈweʦ]

| name (first name) | имя (с) | [ˈimʲa] |
| surname (last name) | фамилия (ж) | [faˈmilija] |

relative	родственник (м)	[ˈrotstwenik]
friend (masc.)	друг (м)	[druk]
friendship	дружба (ж)	[dˈruʒbə]

partner	партнёр (м)	[partˈnɜr]
superior (n)	начальник (м)	[naˈtʃaʎnik]
colleague	коллега (м)	[kaˈlegə]
neighbors	соседи (мн)	[saˈsedi]

4. Human body

body	тело (с)	[ˈtelə]
heart	сердце (с)	[ˈserʦe]
blood	кровь (ж)	[krɔfʲ]
brain	мозг (м)	[mɔsk]

bone	кость (ж)	[kɔstʲ]
spine (backbone)	позвоночник (м)	[pazvaˈnotʃnik]
rib	ребро (с)	[ribˈrɔ]
lungs	лёгкие (мн)	[ˈlɔhkie]
skin	кожа (ж)	[ˈkɔʒə]

head	голова (ж)	[galaˈva]
face	лицо (с)	[liˈʦɔ]
nose	нос (м)	[nɔs]
forehead	лоб (м)	[lɔp]
cheek	щека (ж)	[ɕiˈka]

mouth	рот (м)	[rɔt]
tongue	язык (м)	[jaˈzɪk]
tooth	зуб (м)	[zup]
lips	губы (мн)	[ˈgubɪ]
chin	подбородок (м)	[padbaˈrɔdak]

ear	ухо (с)	[ˈuhə]
neck	шея (ж)	[ˈʃəja]
eye	глаз (м)	[glas]
pupil	зрачок (м)	[zraˈtʃɔk]
eyebrow	бровь (ж)	[brɔfʲ]
eyelash	ресница (ж)	[risˈnitsə]
hair	волосы (мн)	[ˈvɔlasɪ]

hairstyle	причёска (ж)	[pri'ʧoskə]
mustache	усы (м мн)	[u'sɪ]
beard	борода (ж)	[bara'da]
to have (a beard, etc.)	носить	[na'sitʲ]
bald (adj)	лысый	['lɪsɪj]

hand	кисть (ж)	[kistʲ]
arm	рука (ж)	[rʊ'ka]
finger	палец (м)	['paleʦ]
nail	ноготь (м)	['nɔgatʲ]
palm	ладонь (ж)	[la'dɔɲ]

shoulder	плечо (с)	[pli'ʧɔ]
leg	нога (ж)	[na'ga]
knee	колено (с)	[ka'lenə]
heel	пятка (ж)	['pʲatkə]
back	спина (ж)	[spi'na]

5. Clothing. Personal accessories

clothes	одежда (ж)	[a'deʒdə]
coat (overcoat)	пальто (с)	[paʎ'tɔ]
fur coat	шуба (ж)	['ʃubə]
jacket (e.g., leather ~)	куртка (ж)	['kʊrtkə]
raincoat (trenchcoat, etc.)	плащ (м)	[plaɕ]

shirt (button shirt)	рубашка (ж)	[rʊ'baʃkə]
pants	брюки (мн)	[b'ryki]
suit jacket	пиджак (м)	[pi'dʒak]
suit	костюм (м)	[kas'tym]

dress (frock)	платье (с)	[p'latje]
skirt	юбка (ж)	['jupkə]
T-shirt	футболка (ж)	[fʊd'bɔlkə]
bathrobe	халат (м)	[ha'lat]
pajamas	пижама (ж)	[pi'ʒamə]
workwear	рабочая одежда (ж)	[ra'bɔʧija a'deʒdə]

underwear	бельё (с)	[bi'ʎjo]
socks	носки (мн)	[nas'ki]
bra	бюстгальтер (м)	[bys'gaʎtɛr]
pantyhose	колготки (мн)	[kal'gɔtki]
stockings (thigh highs)	чулки (мн)	[ʧul'ki]
bathing suit	купальник (м)	[kʊ'paʎnik]

hat	шапка (ж)	['ʃʌpkə]
footwear	обувь (ж)	['ɔbʊfʲ]
boots (cowboy ~)	сапоги (мн)	[sapa'gi]
heel	каблук (м)	[kab'luk]
shoestring	шнурок (м)	[ʃnʊ'rɔk]

shoe polish	крем (м) для обуви	[krem dʎa 'ɔbʊwi]
gloves	перчатки (ж мн)	[pir'tʃatki]
mittens	варежки (ж мн)	['variʃki]
scarf (muffler)	шарф (м)	[ʃʌrf]
glasses (eyeglasses)	очки (мн)	[atʃ'ki]
umbrella	зонт (м)	[zɔnt]

tie (necktie)	галстук (м)	['galstʊk]
handkerchief	носовой платок (м)	[nasa'vɔj pla'tɔk]
comb	расчёска (ж)	[ra'ɕɜskə]
hairbrush	щётка (ж) для волос	['ɕɜtka dʎa va'lɔs]

buckle	пряжка (ж)	[p'rʲaʃkə]
belt	пояс (м)	['pɔis]
purse	сумочка (ж)	['sʊmatʃkə]

6. House. Apartment

apartment	квартира (ж)	[kvar'tirə]
room	комната (ж)	['kɔmnatə]
bedroom	спальня (ж)	[s'paʎɲa]
dining room	столовая (ж)	[sta'lovaja]

living room	гостиная (ж)	[gas'tinaja]
study (home office)	кабинет (м)	[kabi'net]
entry room	прихожая (ж)	[pri'hɔʒaja]
bathroom (room with a bath or shower)	ванная комната (ж)	['vannaja 'kɔmnatə]
half bath	туалет (м)	[tʊa'let]

vacuum cleaner	пылесос (м)	[pɪle'sɔs]
mop	швабра (ж)	[ʃ'vabrə]
dust cloth	тряпка (ж)	[t'rʲapkə]
short broom	веник (м)	['wenik]
dustpan	совок (м) для мусора	[sa'vɔk dʎa 'mʊsarə]

furniture	мебель (ж)	['mebeʎ]
table	стол (м)	[stɔl]
chair	стул (м)	[stʊl]
armchair	кресло (с)	[k'reslə]

mirror	зеркало (с)	['zerkalə]
carpet	ковёр (м)	[ka'wɜr]
fireplace	камин (м)	[ka'min]
drapes	шторы (ж мн)	[ʃ'tɔrɪ]
table lamp	настольная лампа (ж)	[nas'tɔʎnaja 'lampə]
chandelier	люстра (ж)	['lystrə]

| kitchen | кухня (ж) | ['kʊhɲa] |
| gas stove (range) | газовая плита (ж) | ['gazavaja pli'ta] |

electric stove	электроплита (ж)	[ɛlektrapli'ta]
microwave oven	микроволновая печь (ж)	[mikraval'nɔvaja petʃ]
refrigerator	холодильник (м)	[hala'diʌnik]
freezer	морозильник (м)	[mara'ziʌnik]
dishwasher	посудомоечная машина (ж)	[pasʊda'mɔetʃnaja ma'ʃine]
faucet	кран (м)	[kran]
meat grinder	мясорубка (ж)	[misa'rʊpkə]
juicer	соковыжималка (ж)	[sɔkavɪʒɪ'malkə]
toaster	тостер (м)	['tɔster]
mixer	миксер (м)	['mikser]
coffee machine	кофеварка (ж)	[kafe'varkə]
kettle	чайник (м)	['tʃajnik]
teapot	чайник (м)	['tʃajnik]
TV set	телевизор (м)	[tile'wizɑr]
VCR (video recorder)	видеомагнитофон (м)	['widea magnita'fɔn]
iron (e.g., steam ~)	утюг (м)	[u'tyk]
telephone	телефон (м)	[tile'fɔn]